The
Voodoo
Buddha

Southeast & East Asian Verse

Scott Shaw

Buddha Rose Publications

Library of Congress Control Number:
2012932370

ISBN: 1-877792-56-X
ISBN-13: 978-1-877792-56-4

10 9 8 7 6 5 4 3 2 1

Printed in the United States of America

The
Voodoo
Buddha

Contents

Intro

For all those of you who know me, (or know of me), you know I've spend a lot of time out there in the outback – lost deep, (or deeply), in the abstract realms of Asia. I was first drawn there by *lust for enlightenment.* But, enlightenment came easy for me. It seems instantly, from virtually the moment I entered *The Spiritual Path,* I understood the understanding of Zen, *"That we all are already enlightened. We simply need to remember this fact."* Me, I remembered very young... So, by the time I got there, (Asia that is), that lust had subsidized.

I remember being very sick in India from dysentery at one point in time, I was writing in my journal, questioning my need to be there at all. But, being there, (India), it is kind of like a requirement; a prerequisite, if you will for those of us who walk *The Spiritual Path.* So, there I was... But, I also left; finding/realizing something that I had long understood, (known before I ever arrived), *enlightenment is everywhere.* You don't have to go India, or anywhere else for that matter, to connect or reconnect with it.

And, more than just that... Enlightenment comes in and from many abstract instigators; most are undefined – many never spoken about in holy texts, (at least not the holy texts that are commonly bantered about as holy). In short, you don't have to live in a monastery or a cave to find/experience it. Many/most do not understand this... Those who want to/wish to pass judgment based upon individualized and societal programming and ego, (your ego is not your amigo). Those/they question how can one be spiritual and live a life based in the material world. Well, it is quite simply... Like the old Zen adage states, *"Before enlightenment chop wood carry water. After enlightenment, chop wood carry water."* So, in the case of an individual who has lived a life like I have lived, *"Before enlightenment, live hard, drink hard, love hard. After enlightenment, live hard, drink hard, love hard."*

In any case and etcetera… Instantly, from the moment I arrived, I felt at home in Asia. Some place(s) and some lo-cal(s) more than others. But, I dug *'em* all just the same. This led me to frequently and continually return.

The words you will find in these pages are taken from the notebook(s) that accompanied me to Asia. Notebook(s)… Something I have carried with me everywhere since the *way-back-when.*

I scribed the words that make up these pages in such places as airports, airplanes, hotel rooms, coffee houses, restaurants, bars, in taxis, and on subways.

For lack of a better term, we will call what makes up these pages, *"Poetry."* Writing(s) about time, space, mind, desire, lust, feelings, people, *nirvana,* and all of the etcetera thereof and therefore.

I'll provide you with the place where the writing(s) were written. From this, it may give you a bit of context to the experience(s) that were taking place at a specific point/place in the time of my life.

Well, that's the story. Read on…

Scott Shaw
Bangkok, Thailand
December 1988

the
.................VOODOO
................BUDDHA
verse

no, I don't feel
      sight is my vision
no, I don't feel
      numbed by the drink
      numbed by life
      numbed by the postures of the posers
      numbed
            as the music pounds
            in my ears
                  too loud to describe

but take it away
and it is gone

feel it
      the emptiness
feel it
      the pain
feel it
      the confusion
but hold it
      the dream

and
yes
      this is it
life
      is all that we know

it is here
as I am here
      feelings
      take them away

and the lose
it is felt
    in all of its
    in all of mine
        unfeelingness

so order the wine
    the best
    in this first-class flight
        bastion of sin
    and dream…
        for a feeling
    dream…
        for an end

an end to the beginning
a beginning to the end
    a better place to be
    something more to feel
        other than the zero

I scream
I cry
I try

    I desire it was different
        better/more
something more
    than the felling-less-ness

LAX to Narita

the burn of the grape
as it reaches the lips
touches the tongue
      passive submission
      promised obliteration

      so sweet/so fleeting
      let me know its embrace

LAX to Narita

three

twelve cups of the java down
better make that thirteen
thirteen at forty thousand feet
and the dream
just begin(s) to be lived

LAX to Narita

four

live
and yes it does promise illusion

a secret
known only to the dreamer/known only to the few

sip
champagne/orange juice
        it does go down right

lust
a forty year old Asian lady sits next to me

LAX – NRT
first class flight/first class illusion(s)

as the dream/and the drink take hold

LAX to Narita

three and zero
in Tokyo
she wants to play the romance game
wants to take her time and fall in love
she wants to see if I will wait for her

       sorry babe
       too old for that

so I say goodbye
post a $450.00 meal
       which
       I
       of course
       picked up the tab

so me
I head out into the night
where love has a price tag
and waiting is a game
       left only for the fools

       live it/love it

but I take a moment
       …this moment
I sit down
and write this…
       street kid
       turned street adult
       via a minor monk-hood

but it
but this
but me
it casts me to the wind
      for no one calls street wisdom
           holy
      just as no one call me
           an American fool in Tokyo
           a king

Tokyo

she asks me
     what is your work
I tell her
     I am a dreamer
she laughs
I smile/I continue…
     it is a very difficult job

     yet the truth
     be told
     my words are true
     they are no joke

for the fool's world
it holds control
takes your time/takes your mind
makes most want to be
just like everyone else

me, I never wanted that
never wanted any of that !
but, it (sometimes) does make me question
my reason(s) for
     why

     once, I thought
     how lost I am
     how I do not know
     where to turn
     than/then I realized
     how all those people
     who think that they know

who they are
know where they are going
they are the one(s)
who have nothing/know nothing at all
'cause it can all be gone in a moment

yeah, it is difficult to be a dreamer
where acceptance only comes from the wind
but when the skies hold the laughter
and the clouds cry down the rain
and when the wind is blowing
through my hair
I have no doubt
of who
and what I am

Tokyo

seven

the hours they wash
into the dispassion of waiting

      time moves slowly
          zero can only equal zero

and nothing moves
      how many times have I tried to make it move ?

so moments tick
I watch their action
      this moving scene
      I listen
      hear the words/hear the sounds

and in a lifetime spent
      so short a time
      the hours wash
      to the wasteland of nothing

waiting…

Narita

eight

I sit
in amidst the masses
their noise hums
in a thousand languages
      I
      inadvertently
      walked past
      the *First Class Lounge*
      Fuck !
      I missed it
      it is hidden over to the side
      I pass through passport control
            no going back

but my flight is announced over the loud speaker
so there was no time to melt into the leisure
anyway…
      the flight
      for beyond
      the beyond
            beyond here
            gate' gate' para sam gate' bodhi swaha

no
I am not going home
I am going deeper
deeper
deeper
into the lost realms of Asia

Narita

the G.I.
dressed in civilian rags
and sprouting his mega *bitchin'*
short *do'*
well
he is a *boog-a-looing*
to some sound in his head
      ear plugs
        plugged in deep
he dance to the rhythm
      inside
      the external airport crowd

he takes out the tape
from his portable tape player unit
he flips it over
puts it back in
pushes play
and again
he is lost
to dances of another day
a younger day
another time
a freer time
      his dance/dances on

and then there
      over there…
a slightly plump
but a bit more than babish
of a babe
      dressed all in black
      local Japanese chick

she
dances/moves/sways
to a sound in her head
she too
is plugged in
plugged up tight

so me
I grab my headphones
push them deeply into my ears
push play
and turn the sound
        way up

I close my eyes
I am with them
        moving/grooving
in this international airport
a gateway to the world
I hear no sound
but the sound
the only sound
worth listening to
the sound
pounding through my headphones
        the beat
        that pounds my feet

Narita

they could not know
that my eyes are closed
hidden by my sunglasses

they can not know
I do not hear their words
as my head boobs
to the beat
filling my ears

eyes closed
no one knows
the world
is alien
to me

the move
the talk
the rumbling of a plane in the sky
I sit
in darkness
the only illumination
that of the memories
that of the sound
      eyes closed
      I prefer it that way

Narita to Hong Kong

eleven

a hooker
w/ a cellular phone
      for $700.00 a pop

I can see how she
      pays the bills

I hand her my credit card
I'm willing to pay
she's obviously willing to be paid

here's my credit card.
just a minute. let me call it in.

bid placed
who is the fool
      her
      for her occupation
      or me
      for being willing
      to pay for the moment

and life
what is the answer
      to desire
      to love
      to embrace the emptiness
         and claim it as mysticism
      to fear
      to live
      or to die w/out living

so I lay down the payment
put it on my plastic passion
to be paid for another day

laid down
money
these words
this
her
and
I

me
I only exist
out here
      out here
      on the outskirts
living it
for whatever it is worth

hooker
and a cellular phone
she pulls it out of her purse
      as she calls
      to confirm my payment is real
      as she does
      she gets a beep
      a beep
      on her beeper
            another job/another place
            another dick to please

I smile/I laugh
      but only to myself

then we prepare
      she pulls back the covers
      on my $300.00 a night
      hotel room
      king sized bed

      she takes off her black dress

            in Asia
            hookers always wear black

      she looks to me
I take off my clothes
            no real romance
            just needed preparation
            for a fuck

      she lays down
I lay down
and the rest
it all comes
so naturally

I fuck her good
I fuck all hookers good
            give them something to remember
            give them a reason
            to ask the question
            why

she cums
she cums hard
me too
I cum too

    the deed
    it has been done
    the act of sin
    is complete

    but me
    I feel no shame
    I will ask for forgiveness
    some other day

god damn
she was good
I ask her to marry me
    she says
    yes
    yes we can

    she tells me
    she will call me tomorrow

    call me
    from her cellular phone
    I guess

and then she is gone

    I smile as she walks out the door
    another job to do

I laugh
  out loud
    to myself
all that is left
  are these few words
  for the memory
    for the moment
    of that memory

  yeah
  it/she was worth
  every cent...
  of the seven-hundred bucks

  I think back to L.A.
  my cellular phone
  waits for me there
  I think of my cellular bill
  that I forgot to pay before I left
    how am I going to pay for it
    my cellular bill
    that is
  pay for it out here
    long lost/long gone

    I guess I will figure that out
    some other day

god damn
my life is strange

Hong Kong

twelve

it smells like sex
in this hotel room
    the smell it chases me
    follows me around
        reminds me
of a $700.00 hooker
of a $300.00 a night room
of a pounding
    unforgiving passion

    an answer
        no, there is not one

    a promise
        doubtful

    a message for the masses
        no way, José

so the night moves on
    haunting me
while the sounds of Hong Kong
    pound
    from the streets
    twenty-five stories below
        and me
        I just run
        somewhere to nowhere
        spreading
        plastic passion
           money I do not have

and it all
just doesn't seem to matter
no, not anymore
nothing
anymore
no
not anymore

Hong Kong

so few
can ever know
the dreams
of a drunken fool
they can never see
        never see me
so few
will ever know
the desire for illusion

        a scream
        while you are crying
                into the night
                for the night
                it holds the mysteries
                within its darkness

                and hallowed ground
                it holds
                the truth
                within every lie
                it knows the answer
                within every dream
                        it holds the key

so show me
a surreal meaning
        metaphysics
        by any other name
give me a ticket
to when tomorrow
can never know
the pain of today

if you can't find that location
        give me any ticket
        any-way

Hong Kong

and yeah
I have seen you before
somewhere
out there
in *never-never-land*
and then
as now
I didn't pay your price
I was not willing
to pay
a price too high

the surprise
then
as now
after things
matured/moved
post
the nursing of
the drink/the dream
it came to me
that the price is never too high
no
not out here
in the abyss
the lost mind
of time/space
out here
where only the ethereal
dwell
out here
out here

so I move to the right
yes I see
that they
like you
like I
await the dream
await
the night

just a week out of L.A.
a week
so short
so long
            it all depends how/who
            is living that week
because out here
life is lived fast
life is lived hard
out here
dreams turn to reality
where they may
become something more

but my chance passed
so goodnight to you
all the pagan drunken dreamers
who are here
in this upscale Hong Kong Bar with me
says the same
someone else has grabbed you
paid your price
left me with nothing
but these words

these words
drunkenly scribed in my notebook
that I forever carry in my pocket
  will I even be able
  to read them tomorrow
an echo rattles my mind

so this is for you
for all the ladies
who stare at me
stare into my dream

   dreams in Hong Kong
   dream
   as I dream
   of you
   dream
   as there is nothing more to do

and when the dream
it has been had
it
like the drink
takes you to where
it doesn't matter anymore

no
nothing
matters
anymore

           Hong Kong

moving on
into the unspoken night
the drunken poetry
screams in my mind
drunken poetry
that I forget
to write down

somewhere
lost
on
some
spiritual
horizon
that poetry is recorded
to the *akashic record*

somewhere it exists
somewhere
but no
not here

dream
drunken poet
dream

Hong Kong

oh, the babe
she was barefoot

barefoot
she walked the halls
barefoot
she entered my room
barefoot
she made down my bed

oh, the babe
she was barefoot

now
this is Thailand
where you can have
anything that you want
you known
that you can have it all
       fashion
       and passion

       screams
       and all the dreams

       even a babe
       who comes to your room
       to pull down your covers
       barefoot

I sat there stunned
as she did her job

I sat there stunned
        in love

I told here
        you are beautiful

        she laughed
        I laughed

but this
five-star plus
hotel room
came alive

I asked her
        would you like to come to America with me?

she said
        but I love Thailand

so do I
so do I...

        awh…
        a maid
        she was beautiful
        she was barefoot
        and she loved/lived
        Thailand
        who could argue with that

                        Bangkok

seventeen

I could write the words
saying those things
that I have said before
I could cry the tales of:
        loneliness
        love
        desire
        lust
        enlightenment
but
I believe
I will choose
to remain
Asian silent for now
        I will simply let the clouds
        fill my vision
        as they dance through the sky
I will save these pages
for more worthy vision(s)
        stimulated by:
        lived
                loneliness
        lived
                love
        lived
                desire
        lived
                lust
        live
                enlightenment

Bangkok to Singapore

life in L.A.
    the city
    of one night stands

    and she had a few of them
    or maybe not...

    her stories
    they always seem to change

    then, me
    I came along
        far too late
        I guess

        far too late
        or far too early

        one way or the other
        the right time
        it was not

but you... you are my daydream...

those were the last words
that she said to me
as I hung up the telephone
canceling her
international track me down
telephone call

I called the desk
hold all my call

forever
her dream/not mine

her/my
main and current L.A. babe
she wanted
a large rock
for her finger
to show off
to all of her
Chinese relatives

she wanted
a boob job
      breasts fixed
      to recall a time
      when they were
      "cute and perky"
      a time when
      others knew her
      a time when
      I did not

I met her
I was there
I was asked to fix the damage
      damage
      of a thousand
      past loves/past lovers
all there
before
I even knew her name

I met her
I was there
asked to replace
all her sins
with the words
        forever more
forever
a word
I never understood

we won't end up like them
so she would say to me

                words
                in reference
                to others
                others
                who-were
                one-time
                full-on
                lovers

they had all gone bad

all I have ever seen
by all those
who say the word
        forever
is they all end up
just the same
                love gone to stagnation
                love gone bad
                love gone to nothing

love
left to foolish attachment
boredom
and sex
once a week

the magic
it is all eventually lost
gone to where it began
never-never-land

but I think of her
as I sit here
on this warm
Southeast Asian night

I think of her
and I am glad
that I ran away

ran away
to where the dreams
they are haveable
and the possibility of
           everything/anything
it is at hand
where moments
create new feelings
and what once was
"cute and perky"
never becomes lost
to a boob job
and a diamond ring

no
I would rather
sip from this cup of illusion
than throw my life
down the forgotten tube of forever more

Singapore

there she sits
in all her beauty
all her elegance
        or lack thereof

expensive French restaurant
on Singapore soil
        Chinese and Singaporean
        her beauty
        strikes out against the night

she holds a cigarette in one hand
sips an orange juice
from a straw
stuck in the side of her mouth

beauty
it is
as they say
        only skin deep

her soup arrives
she bends her face
very low over it
slurps it into her mouth

I watch her
as there is nothing better to do

        she attacks it
        engaged
        it is all gone in a heart beat

then the main course
of the main meal
        it is brought on

she eats
        fast/hard
        conquer/kill
she eats it
while she speaks to her friend
with her mouth
        wide open
        full of food

now, it is not
that I am so judgmental

nor is it
that I really care

this is just a story to tell you
a poem to write
of how love/lust
blatantly dies
because no one
ever taught her
that eating is an art
or/and
how to eat with style

Singapore

her Chinese image
blends hard
into the baking scenery
of a blistering hot night

look
there is nothing else
worth looking at
nothing else
in my field of vision
that could mean
a god damned thing

I stare
into/onto her beauty
as Singapore's night
comes down hard

the wine
it is my friend
      red
      expensive
      caressing

and as I stare on
and as I drink on
I realize
how it has the effect/affect
of an ever-increasing
soft focus
      diffusion filter
on the optical spectrum
of life

eye contact
    a smile
        here or there
what do they mean
what can they mean

it is the wine
that touches my lips
not her
    as her vision
    fades farther and farther away
    deep and distant
    into the fading realities
    of life
    driven by the wine
    red
    expensive

I guess tonight
I will choose it
over you
    goodbye
    my fading lady

Singapore

somehow
it is the same scene
in a different land
be it
one side of the earth
or the other

somehow
it is a picture
seen before
      drawn before
      I have looked at it
      one too many times
      and it no longer
      holds its allure

under developed/development

words for poverty
they all mean the same

uncivilized/civilization

speaking in a paradox
where can it lead to

so I walk around
as I have done before
      in so many lands before
I look around
      the sights they are the same

maybe it is I
      far more tainted
      far less adventurous
I look around
      the sights
      they are the same

maybe it is I
      but this same old story
      of third world development
      well, for me…
      it just has lost its appeal

Jakarta

it is not that I woke up
and I was old
nor did I turn around
and my youth was gone
no, I have seen age coming
knowing/watching
its every step forward

      so I have known it
      so I have seen it coming on
      it has taken its toll
      just like on those
      who never witnessed its approach

      it will win
      I cannot

so the past years
I kiss you goodbye
save for a moment or two
that I cast to the realms of literature

      the time
      it goes on
      it will go on

            love and lies
            tears and whys
            time
            it holds all control

Jakarta

tourists
I hate 'em
      westerners
      they think
      that they are so bold
      so much better
            they look down
            on all the locals around them

      they wear tee shirts
      they wear short pants
      sandals and cameras
      they try to get prices lower
      order cheap food
      wear fake imitation watches
            fuck that

I was sitting
in this little indoor/outdoor restaurant
you know the kind
doors wide open
      indoor
      ceiling fan spinning
      outdoor
      tables skirting the street

me
I was sitting back with all my style
      clocking the day
when this guy and his babe
far too underdressed
arrive

he wore this ugly
fake copy of Gucci watch
he sent back a drink
saying it was not
the certain brand of scotch
he ordered
I wanted to laugh
laugh out loud at him
tell him what an asshole
he really was
but I just chilled
        let life live its life

tourists
I hate them
they try to down-play the locals
they think they are so much better
but they are nothing more
than the fools
walking in a fool's shoes
as a fool steps
on a foreign soil

they are the ones
that should be looked down upon

Jakarta

awh shit…
life
it is nothing
$200.00
on a semi-fat
short
none-too-pretty
Indonesian whore

    I can't stop laughing

laughing
    at the horror of it all
laughing
    at the ridiculousness
    of desire
laughing
    at who I am
laughing
    because
    life is such a fucking joke

    it means nothing
    it all adds up to nothing

    and for me
    there is nowhere
    left to run
    nowhere left
    to scream for the dream
    because
    I've already been everywhere

I even fucked
this ugly Indonesian whore
because there was nothing better
to do with my time

Jakarta

.

twenty-five

I stare out my hotel room window
elevated
yes
I suppose it is very high
      by local standards
      at least

I look out
and the night
it is not electric
no, not like Tokyo

it is dark
      dark
      for this is Java

I stare out at it
looking for light
but there is none

I stare out at it
after having been massaged
by the drink
by a lady
but there is no light

no light
in the meaningless caresses of it all
no light
but enlightenment
      all like a Zen Koan

seeing the meaning
in the meaninglessness
in the zero meaning

a zero statement
in a abstract zero world
this is Zen
this is the essence of Zen

so I look out the window
the night
it is dark
I dream of the memories
of all the nights
in Tokyo
and I am glad
that tomorrow
I will be moving back in that direction
away from here
the bottom of the
Southeast Asian world
      leaving here/going there
      moving in a reversal of direction
      back to electricity
      back towards the Tokyo night

I stare out
of my hotel room window
I see the darkness
which exists outside

Jakarta

twenty-six

I kiss you hello
I kiss you goodbye
all without our lips ever meeting

a glance
yes it was a very distant glance
a view of avoidance
as our eyes first
fell into each others

a smile
a vague smile of illusion
the second time
of the only two times
that we ever saw one another

      I would place you
      thirty-ish
      Chinese bloodline
      Java soul

      I would place you
      longing
      yet not knowing
      quite what for

      and into your visionary field
      steps a dream
          long blonde hair
          earrings
          also coming up on thirties
              fast

seeking
yes, seeking
desiring
yes, desiring
longing
yes, longing
and yet
not knowing
quite what for

and there you were
(there she was)
just the way I like 'em
    black hair
    jet black hair
    unshaven legs and underarms

    what has taken civilization
    millions of years to refine
    I choose it lose
    unrefined
    I prefer it natural

but it was all
only for a moment
    a crossing of mind
    a crossing of time
but the fantasy
of our possibilities
it will go on
    forever
    forever more

I know the words
that I would say
if we were
to ever meet again
but it did not happen
      I went
      I looked for you
      I looked to encounter
      your drifting smile
      once again
      but I did not meet your eyes

so now
I am gone
and the memory of you
is placed
to the *akashic* filing cabinet
of all those loves
that should have been
should have touched me
but never did
      filed/folded
      placed away
      for another dream
      on another day

and I am sure
that you will end up
in the arm's of another man
far less worthy that I

Jakarta

twenty-seven

I expected more
I believed more
        to be coming
than a momentary
$200.00
not so worthy whore

I thought more
        was to come of Indonesia
        than has come

maybe it was ten years ago
eight or nine
anyway
but she was there
I was there
we touched
the first Indonesian form
next to mine
        she was scared
                yet beautiful
        she was lost
                yet she believed

        believed in where she was
        she was Indonesian
        I was not
                that was a long-long time ago

now
in truth
by the means
of standards and measures

62

I am still
upon Indonesian soil

it is late
late night/early morning
sometime around three
        pushing four
        in the AM
                my time
                my night

my fight
is leaves in seven hours
so I suppose
that there is still time

but I look out across the night
        it is empty
I look across my hotel room
        piercing high
        into the sky
                it is the same/empty

I look into my soul
        alone
as it has always been

Indonesia
I believed
that you would offer me more

Jakarta

twenty-eight

funny
I look in the mirror
　　a framed image
　　like a photograph

and there/here I sit
　　haveable
　　yet
　　unhad

　　living
　　to no one
　　else's eyes

　　the perfect
　　form of mysticism
　　the only place
　　　　the only station
　　where enlightenment is found

　　enlightenment
　　nirvana
　　famed
　　in
　　a
　　mirror
　　image
　　photograph

Jakarta

this beautiful young
stewardess
walks up to me
as I sit in the first-class lounge
pounding some grape
pounding some java
      java in Java
the breakfast of champions

she comes up
she asks me
are you an actor
I answer
aren't we all

and the rest
      her and I
      is history…

I met her in Java

Jakarta

dreams
of a distant warrior

living is living
only by doing so

life
is lived by availability

take what you can
take what you will

forgotten princesses
calling to the night
     my telephone
     it rings
     in the afternoon

     no way out/no way in
     look
     there is nothing really to see

and as every cry
is caused by every lie
and there really are no answers
to be known

lie
die
live
pay the price

looked for
it cannot be seen
asked for
it is only had

life is a ?

Kuala Lumpur

goodnight Dr. Shaw
I head in my ear

the butler/valet
of my Hilton hotel
      executive floor
      suite
      speaks to me
      as I enter my room
      post dinner

I laugh
to myself
      not yet…
for it is only 10:00 PM
the night is young
      the night is for screams
      it awaits me
      waits for my presence

      I sit back in the abstract
      thoughts of time/life/*satori*
      for a moment
      in its moment-less-ness
            study my life
            my life situation
            listen to classical music
            on a classical music
            hotel room
            radio station

      post a bottle of the grape
      over dinner

red, of course
Italian, of course
I slam down
a cup
no two
no three
of some room service java
as I await the moment of motion
the time when I feel it is right
to enter the night

it comes
it is here
I allow
the scream
to commence
I stand up
I put on my dark blue Italian made
      very-baggy
            suit coat
matching my dark blue Italian made
      very-baggy
            suit pants
I slip on my clunky (big) saw-toothed shoes
I'm ready

the goddess of this night has called me
      called me out
            I enter
            her realm

Kuala Lumpur

oh, you are one of the most beautiful women that I have ever seen and I have been to India, China, and now Malaysia...

an aussie raps
to his bought and paid for date

      it almost makes me sick

love
lust
money
and time
it all equals fucking nothing
and words
they mean nothing at all

so I listen
because I can't help but hear
his voice is loud
as if to try to impress somebody
      somebody
      when nobody
      cares

everybody knows
he is with a whore

but I listen
      ...am forced to
as I complete the bottle of Italian vino

I finish my dinner
I finish my desert
I walk forward
and outwards
feeling the percussion
of the night

rap(s)
I've heard them all
and the truth be told
I have laid down plenty myself
      but maybe its age
      maybe it is wisdom
      but for those aussie tourist losers
      who order wine by the glass
      keep their elbows on the table
      own only one cheap suit
      and never wear it
      I don't need to hear it
      the words, that is
      spoken to a lady
      who has heard them all before
      done it all before
            give me dinner in silence
            love away from fear
            nighttimes
            that go on forever and ever
            and wine
            red and Italian
            if you please

Kuala Lumpur

old man
sitting in a Malay discothèque
      leave
      and
      die
      it would be better for all of us

leave the dance
leave the room
for the young

the bar
is full of them
married/childrened
wives for sure
      far off in the distance
      in western land(s)
      that the local(s)
      can only dream
      of visiting

the bar is full
the men who make up this bar
their pockets are full
      of bargaining and debates
      for the young ladies
      that they wish to buy

their clothing is casual
cheap
they are rude to the waitress
I am ashamed
that they are
of my race

old men
in a Malay disco

     in the States
     in L.A.
     if they were on my turf
     they would be laughed at
     laughed out of the place
     but here
     their money
     the illusion they hold
     simply by being white
     speaks more
     than their age
     and their lack of style

go home
go back
leave the dancing
to the young
leave the nights
to the free

Kuala Lumpur

thirty-four

I love good wine
I love good women
    drunken
    ah yes
    drunken

    kiss me
    oh, the kiss
    it is so sweet
    give me a new reason
    give me the difference
    of your lips
    different from the ones
    last night
    give me
    your reason
    I am sure
    yours is different

love and lust
death and love
    equals
    equals
    equals
    nothing
        nothing at all

the way you speak
of being Chinese
speak of being Chinese
    in Malaysia
makes all the difference in the world

difference
you are different
I am different
how the difference(s)
fuel the world

she wants to save her race
        but
she wants to be with me
        race is gone
        love is coming on
                life
                and lust
                the promises of nothing

as the drunken poet
lives his life
out here
in the outback
out here
on the outskirts

        those
        who know/understand
        no mind
        give me the night(s)
        give me the lust
        give me the dream
        in a drunken state
        induced by the wine
        give me the space
        to live this dream
        with this drunken

Chinese/Malaysian girl
who desires
our lips to meet
      and meet the do

Kuala Lumpur

thirty-five

I love the vibration
the feeling
as the drunken ground
      it shakes
      it moves

but it is not real
I am not real
      no, not at all

talk
it is for the nothing
sound
it vibrates the nothing

a hundred years
of a world
w/ no answer(s)
I live this lunch of illusion
I love to live

Kuala Lumpur

om namah shivah
she walked out
as the three A.M. hour
was coming on

om namah shivah
I looked
into her eyes
       the whites were yellow
I looked away
and I saw the red
       the red you see
       like the coming on of acid
          the LSD
       red
       like the burning of the dawn
       new to life
       new to the day
       when everything-everything
       changes
       and becomes new

om namah shivah
like the words
my guru of the enchanted mind
gave me
like the words of an ethereal warrior
taking control of the soul

       and me...
       here I am
       lost deeply
       in the night

I looked away
I tried to make her gone
she did not go away

early worship
of the destroyer
the night
yes, the kisses of the night
  parvati
  sarawsati
  gavatri
  I knew them all

the dark destroyer
blue
in color
she
  this woman
  was like that
  she was *kali* incarnate

yes
she held the kisses of the night
for she was dark
her power was dark
  power
  it is always dark

  dark
  for dark
  find the light
  look for it
  but it can not be seen

me
with nowhere else to run
I allowed her glance
to glance at me
I allow her energy
to take control over me
I allow her body
to merge with mine

I allowed it
but I did not desire it
did not want it to be so
but it was

om namah shivah

Kaula Lumpur

we lay next to each other
awake
      awake
      but we pretend to be asleep

life
it is so empty
love
it is so worthless
naked
      we lie
naked
      we live the lie
for what it was/what we sought
it was never there
we hoped
that it may have been
but
it was not

dark and light
her skin and mine
black to white
nothing to nothing

colors blend
to the night and the light
all in the perception
so we say

into the nothingness
sex
is was zero

feelings
they were zero

we lay next to each other
awake
but pretending to be asleep

Kuala Lumpur

thirty-eight

I see the face(s) around me
sure, I hear their word
     sights and sound

their faces
they look at me
they speak to me
     yelling
in their meaningless speech
     crying
in their meaningless tears
     screaming
         for the dream

me
I scream
as well

Kuala Lumpur

thirty-nine

I feel nothing

    love
    it has come and gone
    again

    infatuation

    love
    it equals nothing

    I feel nothing

this morning I woke up
I turn
I look
I see
this beautiful Chinese/Malaysian girl
laying naked on my bed
next to me

her face
it was covered in tears
the kind/she claims
she does not know how to cry

but me
I am who I am
I telephone the airline
made my reservations
for the exit
which is where
I now sit

I feel nothing

I promised
to love her
I gave her
a momentary dream
she gave me
a momentary nothing

      momentary
      and nothing
      they seem to go
      hand-in-hand

I feel nothing
      no loss
      no gain
      no love

      love
      equals
      nothing

as I make my exit
exit to a darker night
and onto a rising nightmare

it call(s) to me
I have to go
      I feel nothing

Kuala Lumpur

forty

Bangkok
this is the world
lost deeply
in the night

this is where
I am home

I am going to stay here
lose myself
so deeply
never to be found again
never to return again
      the drunken
      streets of darkness
      I smell them
      I feel them
      I hear them
      beating a rhythm
      known only to the few

late into the night
I peer
there is no way out for me
no way in
      only lust
      lust in its purist existence
      its most perfect form

the night
cries to me
it holds me
too tight

too tight
to night
to night
to night
I will never be able to leave

Bangkok

tonight
I leave
for the illusion(s)
the possibilities
of love
      lost in the distance
tonight
I will not wait
to see if it comes
      tomorrow
I throw
the wrench
into the wheel
      live
      lust
      love
paid for
by any means
taken
to any logical limit
      the logic of lust
      where there is none

so come to me tonight
but only if you don't
want to save me for tomorrow
for tomorrow
I will have
nothing left to lose
      come to me
      in all of your passion
      eyes wide open
      mind in action

and tonight
this night
we will call it forever

tonight
tonight

Bangkok

in the dream of the late night
living in the silhouetted images of oblivion
lost in the abstraction
       love is easy
       it comes on so fast

late night:
       post the meeting
       post the pick-up
       post the dancing
       post the drinks
       she takes me back
           back
           to her humble
           five bedroom abode
           and she screaming-ly
           makes love to me

       the night ends
           late
       early in the dawn
           5:00 AM
       the sun is rising
       the light comes in
           hard
           cold
           and silent

       it enters
       like a screaming
       aging virgin
       who lost her one and only change for love
       many-many-many years ago

the ceiling fan
it rotates above me
beating a rhythm
that I can not understand

its movement(s)
hypnotize me
its beat
          screams

I lay there
she lay there
the crystal blue light
of the night
is fading
to the passionate blue
of the oncoming day

          I have never seen
          a color like this before

the ceiling fan
moves
in shadows
as the light
begins to surround us

I am awake
          sleep
          seems
          somehow
          so unimportant

so unnecessary
so unneeded
    living this moment
    is so much more essential

the norm of the passion
the passion we had
and the oncoming heat
of a Bangkok day
    the ceiling fan
        turns
    the cool night
        fades
    a night
    where the heat
    was embraced
    the love
    known
    and lust
    provided needed emancipation

she
the beautiful woman
quietly sleeps
softly next to me

I think of that fact
that maybe our connection
may have been too strong
    but maybe not
    maybe it was destiny
    a moment
    we both needed/desired to live

the birth of us
basking in vision
only know to those
who inhabit
the realms of the late night

our meeting
stabbing
at non-ending
samadhi
the kind that can only be lived
by fools
who inhabit the dream
of a place known only by the liberated

with nothing left to lose
        last night
she leaned over and kissed me
something a Bangkok woman
would never normally do
she kissed me
as others looked on
        sealing our fate

the fan turns
she sleeps
me
I remain lost
in the perfection of this moment
        a body laying next to me
        the hue of blue radiating
        a fan turning overhead
        as the night fades to day

as the cool fades to heat
        Bangkok is always so hot

my mind has gone silent
it is as if
I am dreaming
        in front of my eyes
        the dream moves on
        yet I remain
        alert
        awake
        silent
        lost
        in this deadly sin
        lost in pure mysticism
        my mind
        spins with the fan
        in the lost kiss
        of a lost night

Bangkok

forty-three

it is sad
now illusion fades
so quickly

how illusion
loses itself
so soon

sad
how infatuation
moves to boring melancholy

sad
how the dream lived
turns to the desire of running away

      was she like any other ?
      no
      I don't think so

      did she hold any special traits ?
      no
      not really

      was there any clue
      that would make me want to love her forever ?
      no
      I don't think so

nothing is/so nothing does

her embrace
it held me for a second

I looked
and then it was gone

      maybe it is just that I am far too tainted
           having seen
           far too much
           lived far too long
           in worlds
           which proved to have
           no meaning

           love
           that always goes astray

it is sad
how love fades
to emptiness
sad
how my heart
no longer fills
with emotion
sad
how nothing equals nothing
and a kiss is here
and then it is gone

      I just want
      to walk away

Bangkok

a fan spins
above my head
beating in rhythm
to music
that plays
on the Southeast Asian stereo

I lay back
on the large pillows
I lay back
into her arms
I lay back
still screaming for the dream

looking around
a lizard
is on the wall
I don't want to see it
      I close my eyes
      I put my lips to hers
      kiss her
      hoping that this action
      will solve my dilemma
      hoping that the embrace
      will be the key
      be the answer to my dreams

      but no
      it is nothing
      nothing that has not
      been felt before

the music plays
L.A. sounds
the fan beats
its sacred rhythm
I look around
damn !
there has got to be something more
but there is not

Bangkok

she call me on the late-night telephone
    3:00 AM
    says the clock on the wall

she calls me
want to know
why I have not phoned her
wants to know
when I will return

    she's in K.L.
    I'm in B'kok

    You number one – big time player, I think!
    so she says to me

    What do you mean?
            I question
    I gave that up long ago!

long ago…
long ago…
I have tried, lord
yes, I have tried

but the pounding of my heart
meets the pounding of my feet
and walking away
seems the only alternative
    ever…

    full
    full of what

full of nothing
I tried to love her
I really did !

the late-night telephone rings
Malaysian English
full of slang, *"La."*
it is spoken to me
       I am accused
       I am guilty
       but still I live the dance
              where any dream will do
              any passing fantasy
              is worth its weight in gold

              love lived
              love lost
              what can it mean

3:00 AM
I'm back from my night
Southeast Asian early
       this night
       the telephone rings
       as I enter the door

Malaysia phone call for you, Dr. Shaw.

my alcohol tilted ears hear
but there is nothing to be said
       nothing to be lived
       nothing but the lied
       the lie of more

I would have been fine,
          she states
If you would have just fucked me and went away.
But, you play too well.
You say too much.
You made me feel too much !
Now I can't sleep.
I can't stop thinking of you !"

compound argument
I carry it on
tell her to dream
tell her I love her
tell her to forget
tell her to go to sleep

          this dream
          has gone on
          to another night
          another fantasy
          another lost vision
          of another gone girl
          that I will never see again
          another reason
          to forget the fact
          that I live
          in a world where
          any dream will do
          sorry for living the dream through you

Bangkok

forty-six

I was driven off
deeper into the night
deeper
than I have ever been before

       this was it
       this was serious

lust and longing
fluorescent glow
straight
straight as an arrow
       no, not the sharpest
       no, not the form
       no, not the fullness
       of the deepening glow of Shanghai
       no, this Bangkok
       and here
       depth is scary

       Bangkok
       straight
       long
       hard
       so hot
       it is cold

her legs
they were up against me
were wrapped around me
they were hot as a torch
a lost touch
the lost burning touch of nothing

like a Zen expression
there
but not there
real
but unreal

but none-the-less a ticket
deeper in
deeper on
       no longer
       is there any way out
       I have lost that chance/that option
       I lost it
       long ago

       now
       there is only a deeper way in
       deeper
       into the night

Bangkok

give me the whores
the sluts
the gutter tramps
for they know how to live
        or are at least
                better
                at pretending
I am so fucking tired
of chasing
the vestal virgin dream

the virgins lie
        why is it
        that they all tell me
        that they are a virgin ?

so slap me
w/ your promiscuity
tell me
that you just don't care
tell me
that it all
didn't mean
a fucking thing
        me too
        me too

Bangkok

disco beat pounding
as the jazz
goes down
she was telling me
in some weird dialect
that we can party
but I didn't understand
      at sunrise
      a day later
      I realized what
      she was a-talkin' about

Southeast Asian
five-star bitches
other
that is
than the one
I was cribbed up w/

disco beat crying
I blew it
I didn't understand her
didn't know what she meant
so instead of a new dream
every cent worth living
I'm such her
dick locked up deep
in the old

Bangkok

105

you're playing hard
you're digging yourself in too deep
    run
    or stay
    destiny
    is at hand

    and I cry
    to the ancients
    may it be heard

    living
    is the only antidote

Bangkok

fifty

I
I am
the player supreme

I ask her
    can you read English
she answers
    yes, I can

I hand her the note
pre-prepared especially for her

    would you like to fall in love
    are the words
    printed upon the page

lost in love
no room for vision
lost in wisdom
no time for love
    back and forth
    to and fro
    there is
    no absolute

Bangkok

perhaps
it is only us
      the dreamers
      the thinkers
      the lovers
      the drunks
      and the fools
who can look at one another
and instantly fall in love

perhaps it is us
      the lost
      the confused
            those of us
            with nothing left to lose
who can meet
and know that
length of time
has no importance

but this is for you
my newest Thai love
we held hands
and my heart
      it pounded
we touched
      and my heart it soured
all those feelings…
      feelings I though lost
      long ago

now, I sit here
in the late night
     4:00 AM
     Bangkok time
     and I write
         yes
         this is for you

for out here
on the extremities
women are easy
     the promises
     they are even easier
     and mysticism
     is not hard to find

it is mysticism
that makes me turn
turn and move on
for yes
I could love you
     as momentary
     as that would be
and yes
I could use you
     for your body
     for your feeling(s)
and you could use me as well
     for whatever is left in me to lose

         for my money
             which has become in short supply

for my time
which is aging rapidly
for my mind
for whatever it is worth
use and abuse

but neither of us
could give the other
what we truly need
you, America
me, a dream

so I kissed you on the forehead
one time
I turned to walk away
you grabbed my hand
you leaned back
you looked for our lips to meet
they met
my mistake or yours
only life/only time will tell

I took you to my room
we kissed
we lay upon the floor
I prepare to make love to you

but we're not married

I proceed
I do the deed anyway

rip/tear
life torn
blood everywhere
I ruined her
     I didn't know

     for how many times
     have I been told
       I am a virgin
     when they were not

rip/tear
life torn
blood everywhere
I ruined her
     I didn't know
     had I know/had I believed
     I would not have

     we take a shower
     she catches a *tuk tuk*
     she goes home

me
I do what I do
I slip off
into the early morning daylight
maybe it is better this way
     run
     run away
     it is something I always seem to do

run
because I know
it would only end up
the same
visited so many times in my past
     love
     lust
     fading love
     fading lust
     looking for anything
     anything as opposed to nothing
     seeking any reason to run away

perhaps it is me
     the distance
     the feeling
          unfeeling
     the caring
          uncaring
which leads my world astray

but if this were any other daydream
and not an impending nightmare
I would have stayed
     but it is not
     so I did not
     I turned
     I do what I do
     I left
     I let you live your life
          free of me

Bangkok

love
        the game
        all that's lost and gained

a player supreme
        I was recently titled
a player supreme
        or just a fool

        I gave her a note
        would you like to fall in love ?

        well…

        and in looking down
        there was the note
        held tightly in her hand
        held tightly
        through the night

        this is the answer,
        she said

dressed up for the whores
the heat of Bangkok
pounds down on me
sweet oozes from my veins
it draws the life-force from me
fill me up
once again

dressing up for the whores of Bangkok
put it on
to fully take it off

dressing up for the whores of Bangkok
got it up
to get it in

and the prices
they get paid
exchanged paper
for her pink

who is using who
(or is that whom)
who wins
who loses
in a world like theirs
in a world like mine

I guess it really doesn't even matter

dressing up for the whores
the game
it is worth playing

the game it is worth living
      the game of winners and losers

      like life
      just the zero
      me
      I try to make it
      something more

dressing up for the whores of Bangkok

Bangkok

the dreams die hard
out here
on the far side of midnight
the far side of midnight
where life
it has no meaning
no
none at all

a price
it is paid
a form
it is know
but only for a fleeting moment
had it been any other place
another time
it could have meant
so much more

and you know
this is where the illusion lies
lying
that this life
it adds up to anything at all
yeah, we are this
sure, we are that
and we could have been…
we would have been…
we should have been…
but we are/we were not
and so what…
it all ends up the same
death

so let the dreams fall away
give them to the children

    take what you can get
    give what you feel like giving

    and watch the wind
    blow through the sky

Bangkok

I knew her when…
…when the junk did not hold her
 it had not yet taken control
 over her soul

I knew her when…
…when there still was the promise
 of the dream
 in her eyes
 not just the thought
 of a needle in her veins

 yeah
 I watched it coming
 and there was not a god dammed thing
 that I could do about it

  and the dream
  lives on
  forever and ever
  who she was
  yeah, that's what I still
  hold in my mind

  I watched as the now became nothing
  lost/gone forever
  just waiting until
  the needle comes again
  and steals
  one more piece
  of her life

Yeah, I quit Monday. By Friday I should be able to stand up and walk okay. Then we will go out. Then we can sit and talk about old times Then, I know, my life will be better. Friday, Friday...

Friday never came
back on the junk Thursday
she OD'd
she died
Thursday night

and what does it all mean
what can it all hold
a moment
where it doesn't matter
what we are not
      but that moment
      lead to our last goodbye

sleep well in all your dreams
my sweet lady
they have to be better than the life you lived
see you when there are no more tomorrows
and our souls float free
in the wind

Bangkok

fifty-six

I put my hand to my face
I can still smell the juice of a whore
     a night time of nothing
     something
     just the same

     take the women
     I have taken so many
     they sit behind the glass wall
          I choose the one I want

     me
     they all wave
     point
     want me to choose them
     I guess I look different
     different, than their average client(s)
          long blonde hair
          a baggy Italian suit
          big clunky shoes
          verses
          Japanese Businessmen
          Saudi Sheiks
          Middle-East Oil Barrens
          Thais with a few *bhat* to spend

     take the women
     I have taken so many
     they sit behind the glass wall
     I choose the one I want

     I guess I have taken too many
     I have just become so bored

and the games and the dance
go on and on
and I got no more time
      cast to pagan memories
      lost to her meaningless smile
      and another time/another place
      another decision made

      well, I guess I could have loved her
      if we had met
            another place
            another time
            another way
      no, not really
      I don't believe in love
            just desire
            attachment
            yeah, that's it
            that's what I would have done
but cast to dreams
of this/of that
of the nothing
that I felt
when I touched her
I touched her
for no good reason
no, not any at all
      life is so sad
      I put my hand to my face
      I can still smell the juice of a whore

                                        Bangkok

fifty-seven

the days
they drift here
     Bangkok

          a dream to die
          a realization
          that there is no way home
          no home to return to

and so off I go into the nothing
of the pouring/pounding heat
hope that it will reveal
something/anything to me
     something more than nothing
     the nothing that fills my life

the days
they drift here
Bangkok

                                Bangkok

fifty-eight

mirrors on the wall
got no place to hide
mirrors on the ceiling
got no place to run

yeah, she's got the movement
she learned them all real well

yeah, she got the feeling
life(s) and time(s)
practice, I guess…

I lay on the bottom
letting her do her job
she is up on top
moving
          continually

she looks in the mirror
studies her own face
watches her every move
          like if she is wondering
          just how good she fucks

I would answer her question
if she asked
          yeah, you fuck real good

Bangkok

love starved
love sick
I have left
a long list of fallen treasures
in my Southeast Asian wake

love lost
I have left Bankok
feeling this way before

     and the splinters
     they stab deep

     no way in
     no way out

Bangkok

sixty

I sit here
in the dark
closed in/closed out
I like it that way

the world surrounding me
        turn it down
        turn it off

I would rather hang
with Southeast Asian whores
who know no better
than with Westerns
who act like fools

shut it down
close it down
        shades drawn
        sunglasses on
        beat pounding tight
        in my ears

        check out

Bangkok

sixty-one

Japan
used to be my savior
no longer though
        I believe it to be true

far too tainted
        I have become
far too clean, pristine
        this society lives

leave me somewhere
in Southeast Asia
where the sun and the heat
breaks the soul into submission

where the skin
becomes aged
far before its time

where there is no way out
no way in
only a bleak existence
in a culture
long ago lost
to superstition
        long ago

Tokyo

sixty-two

I roll down the window
the Tokyo night rain
slaps me in the face
     hard
     slow
     and cooling

the summer nights
they have begun

                                          Tokyo

it is raining in Asia
last night as I walked out of the
twenty-four hour hotel lounge
there where
she
she and I discussed
Bangkok love and forever
I looked up
and the first drop of rain
fell upon my head
        love it is easy
        sex it is easy
        running away the easiest
        of them all

I caught an early morning plane to Tokyo
post an
up-all-night
session of nothing
        I'm sure she called it passion
        we fucked all night
        but I call it nothingness
        nothingness lost in the obvious

I walked down from the plane
onto the tarmac
the world
was full of haze
        sterile urbanization
the rain drops
they had followed me
across the continent(s)

what was once a sign
of divine intervention
now
leads only to confusion
and not knowing what to do
        what does it mean?

it is raining in Asia

                                                Tokyo

her eyes
they are not clear
a slight tint of yellow
a slight tinge of red
her skin
shows the age of time
though
in fact
she is two years young than I

life for her
it has not been easy
life
in my Southeast Asian dream
       made for me
       lived by me
       I like those
       whose lives have been hard

       the sun
       scorches the gods
       the heat
       erases vision
       all that is left
       is the yearning
       for where it all went wrong

       the sad thing is
       what she does not/will never know
       is that there is no escape
       from the Southeast Asian angels of demons

I looked at her
the first time I really saw her
instantly, I fell in love
but love is fleeting
    my money
    and the lack of
    drove me/forced me
    to leave
    fly
    Bangkok to Tokyo

but hard and soft
hot and cold
old and young
the never ending female form(s)
it calls me/it forces me
it reminds me of
my reason to return

screaming in the night
if my dollar sign was bigger
I would turn around
I would go back to her
I would love her
    hard

    I like those
    who have lived
    hard
    for they are the one
    who know how to feel

Tokyo

we walked outside
it was 3:00 AM
we had met
two days before

      it/this
      was our first night
      w/ out the walls of society
      between us

we walked outside
and it began to rain
      the sky
      was crying for our love
      for it knew
      that it could never be

Tokyo

a dream
of any other stranger
a place
alone
where any dream will do
    time to run
    time to love
    time to die

    a warrior's cry
    a lover's death
    a rich many poverty
        truth untold
        lies forgotten
        kiss me deadly
        kiss my sins

last night
all night
and the things we never were
home
when you have none
    none and alone
    they seems to go
    hand-in-hand

Tokyo

the air is stagnate
w/ the smell of life

old
everyone
no matter how young
looks
very-very
old

and where does this world
want to go
what is it
that this day
wants to do

people walk
they go to job(s)
      their job(s)
this is their morning
that is what they are doing
god damn doesn't anybody realize
that there is so much more to life
      I guess not…

Taipei

sixty-eight

second cup of the coffee
as the airplane warms up

stare out the window
grey through the glass

grey to grey
light to dark
fly though the night
to the other side of the date line
       I will get to live this day again

to LAX

About the Author

Scott Shaw is a prolific author, actor, artist filmmaker, photographer, and composer. Shaw's poetry and literary fiction were first published by literary journals in the late 1970s. He continued forward to have several works of poetry and literary fiction published, in book form, during the 1980s. By the mid 1980s, after having spent years traveling extensively throughout Asia, documenting obscure aspects of Asian culture in words and on film, his writings on social science began to be published, as well. As the 1990s dawned, Shaw writings, based upon a lifelong involvement with the martial arts and eastern mysticism, began to be embraced. From this, he has authored literally hundreds of articles and a number of books on meditation, the martial arts, yoga, and Zen Buddhism; published by large publishing houses.

Scott Shaw *Books-in-Print* include:

*About Peace: A 108 Ways to Be At Peace
     When Things Are Out of Control*
Advanced Taekwondo
Bangkok and the Nights of Drunken Stupor
Bus Rides
*Cambodian Refugees in Long Beach,
     California: The Definitive Study*
Chi Kung For Beginners
China Deep
E.Q.
Essence: The Zen of Everything
Hapkido: Essays on Self-Defense
Hapkido: The Korean Art of Self Defense
Independent Filmmaking: Secrets of the Craft
Junk: The Backstreets of Bangkok
*Last Will and Testament According to the
     Divine Rite of the Drug Cocaine*
*Marguerite Duras and Charles Bukowski:
     The Yin and Yang
     of Modern Erotic Literature*
Mastering Health: The A to Z of Chi Kung
Nirvana in a Nutshell
No Kisses for the Sinner
On the Hard Edge of Hollywood
*Sake' in a Glass, Sushi with Your Fingers:
     Fifteen Minutes in Tokyo*
Scream: Southeast Asia and the Deam
Samurai Zen
Shanghai Whispers Shanghai Screams
Shattered Thoughts
Suicide Slowly
Taekwondo Basics
Ten to Thiry

The Ki Process:
  Korean Secrets for Cultivating Dynamic Energy
The Little Book of Yoga Breathing
The Little Book of Zen Mediation
The Most Beautiful Woman in Shanghai
The Passionate Kiss of Illusion
The Screenplays
The Tao of Self Defense
The Warrior is Silent:
  Martial Arts and the Spiritual Path
TKO: A Lost Night in Tokyo
Yoga: The Spiritual Aspects
Zen Buddhism: The Pathway to Nirvana
Zen Filmmaking
Zen in the Blink of an Eye
Zen O'clock: Time to Be
Zen: Tales from the Journey

www.ingramcontent.com/pod-product-compliance
Lightning Source LLC
Chambersburg PA
CBHW070944100426
42738CB00010BA/2046